EMC123-Gross and Frightening Animal Facts (eBook)

Mason Crest Publishers 6 Volumes Flipbook
Set Price: $184.32
Reading Level:6th Grade, 7th Grade, 8th Grade
Interest Level: Middle, Secondary
Accelerated Reader: No

High Interest - Fans of intriguing yet disgusting facts about animals will find a great deal to squirm at with squeamish delight in this new stomach-churning series. Each book will engage reader after reader in the most visceral of ways. This series is action packed with fun, brought to life in a presentation of facts, & statistics, accompanied by many, never seen before, jaw dropping pictures throughout. Featuring everything from offensive odors to prehistoric puke, these feral facts are not for the faint-hearted! Combining natural history, science & a sense of humor, these books are sure to keep even the most reluctant readers entertained while they learn.

Title	Code	List Price	Our Price	Copyright	Prg
Bizarre Animals	EMC278611	$30.72	$30.72	2018	
Disgusting Animals	EMC278628	$30.72	$30.72	2018	
Freaky Animals	EMC278635	$30.72	$30.72	2018	
Lethal Animals	EMC278642	$30.72	$30.72	2018	
Scary Animals	EMC278659	$30.72	$30.72	2018	
Stinky Animals	EMC278666	$30.72	$30.72	2018	

GROSS AND Frightening ANIMAL FACTS

FREAKY ANIMALS

Stella Tarakson

MC

MASON CREST

Mason Crest
450 Parkway Drive, Suite D
Broomall, Pennsylvania 19008
(866) MCP-BOOK (toll free)

First printing
9 8 7 6 5 4 3 2 1

ISBN (hardback) 978-1-4222-3926-1
ISBN (series) 978-1-4222-3923-0
ISBN (ebook) 978-1-4222-7863-5

Cataloging-in-Publication Data on file with the Library of Congress

Freaky Animals
Text copyright © 2015 Pascal Press Written by Stella Tarakson

First published 2015 by Pascal Press PO Box 250, Glebe, NSW 2037 Australia

Publisher: Lynn Dickinson Principal Photographer: Steve Parish © Nature-Connect Pty Ltd
Additional Photography: See p. 48 Researcher: Clare Thomson, Wild Card Media Editor: Vanessa Barker

THAT'S FREAKY!

CHAPTER 1

THAT'S FREAKING UGLY!

Some faces are so revolting only a mother could love them—especially when she's just as ugly! Have you ever heard the saying "beauty is in the eye of the beholder"? Keep that in mind, and try not to freak out while you behold these gruesome creatures ...

The proboscis monkey's nose never stops growing. Even when it's telling the truth!

I NOSE IT.

NOSEY

BAGGY

The Titicaca water frog has baggy folds of skin. All wrinkly and creased, its skin looks like a used paper bag!

MY MOTHER LOVES ME!

© NORFANZ Founding Parties/Kerryn Parkinson

SLIMY

What looks like a fat, grumpy old man with a bulbous nose and too much attitude? If you thought "Grandpa," best keep it quiet! It's the blobfish, a slimy pink fish that has to be seen to be believed. The blobfish lives off the southern Australian coast in deep waters. It might not look great, but its blobby body allows it to withstand the high pressures of living at depths of up to 0.6 miles (1 kilometer).

Who you calling UGLY??

The warthog, with its misshapen face and squinty eyes, is certainly no beauty. And its temperament matches its looks! It has lashed people to death with its tusk-like teeth. Fifty years ago, the naturalist Pitman observed, "It is one of the most astonishing objects which has ever disgraced nature; its face seems to have gone all wrong."

WHAT A SWINE!

DIRTY DEEDS

Pollution can do a great deal of harm to animals. This frog is missing an eye!

NICE NAME
SHAME ABOUT THE FACE

The stargazer fish gets its name because it has eyes on top of its head. Unfortunately, this fish isn't as pretty as its name. It has a huge square head and a large, upturned mouth, making it look like a bulldog—and an ugly bulldog at that!

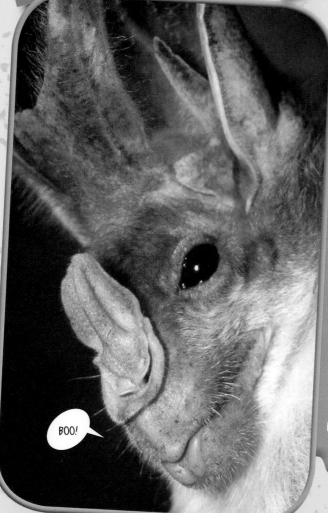

BOO!

BAT UGLY

Would you rather encounter a ghost or a bat? Neither? Then steer clear of the ghost bat. This ugly Australian native gets its name because of its light grey, almost white coloring. It lives mainly in caves and mineshafts in rainforests and arid areas. It is Australia's only carnivorous bat.

COLOR-FREE CREATURES

Albinos are animals whose skin, eyes and fur have no color pigments. They can look white or even pink due to the color of their blood showing through. For wild animals, this rare trait can spell trouble. Unless they live in snow fields, they have trouble hiding from predators. A white animal, for example, can't camouflage itself against a brown tree trunk!

DON'T WORRY — I'M ALL WHITE!

Sea creatures can be albino too! Migaloo is an extremely rare white humpback whale that is regularly sighted migrating up the eastern coast of Australia.

MADE FOR
THE SHADE

Pigments help protect human and animal skin from the harsh rays of the sun. Albinos, of course, can't produce pigments. Too much exposure to UV light can cause bad sunburn—and, in severe cases, can even lead to cancer.

I NEED MORE SUNSCREEN.

ME TOO!

Albino reptiles have it even harder than other colorless animals. As they are cold-blooded, they depend on external heat to regulate their body temperature, but they can easily get badly sunburned. Without enough sunlight, their metabolism—the process by which food is broken down for energy—is disrupted.

CHAPTER 2

FREAKY SENSES

Some people claim to have a sixth sense—but you knew that already, right? Try and predict the freaky senses that some of these animals possess!

Some animals can detect sounds that are so high we can't hear them. Some moths can hear frequencies of up to 300,000 kilohertz. That's about 15 times the highest pitch detectable by humans!

I EARS YA!

While some animals can hear higher sounds than humans, elephants can hear much lower sounds. They make rumbling noises deep in their stomachs. Other elephants can detect the low rumbles across long distances through their feet!

HEARING RANGES

Young adult human	= 20–20,000 Hz
Elderly human	= 50–8,000 Hz
Rat	= 1,000–50,000 Hz
Cat	= 100–60,000 Hz
Dolphin	= 200–150,000 Hz
Elephant	= 1–20,000 Hz
Goldfish	= 5–2,000 Hz
Moth, noctuid	= 1,000–240,000 Hz
Mouse	= 1,000–100,000 Hz
Sea lion	= 100–40,000 Hz
Tuna	= 50–1,100 Hz
Cockatiel	= 250–8,000 Hz
Dog	= 67–45,000 Hz
Blue whale	= 5–12,000 Hz
Humpback whale	= 30–28,000 Hz

Sounds that are too high for humans to detect are called ultrasound. Dog whistles are too high for us to hear but send dogs into a frenzy! Sounds with frequencies below the range of human hearing are called infrasound. Elephant vocalizations are infrasonic, meaning they are too low for humans to hear.

HOT LIPS

Did you know that pythons can "see" heat? They have heat-sensitive pits on their lips. The pits act like infrared detectors to help locate warm-blooded prey. Images are formed in the python's brain, much like vision in the human brain.

TONGUE TASTER

Snakes may not be able to use cutlery, but they have forked tongues to make up for it! They flick their tongues in and out, using them to pick up scent traces. A special organ inside their mouths helps them figure out what the smell is. Having a forked tongue makes it easier to pinpoint exactly where the smell is coming from.

SOMEONE IS HAVING A BBQ!

RIPPLE ALERT

Crocodiles lie in waterholes at night, waiting to ambush animals that come to the water to drink. Crocs have special pressure sensors on their skin that allow them to detect even the slightest motion in the water. They also have great night vision. In full daylight, a crocodile's pupils close to a narrow slit. In the darkness, they open to a full circle to allow in maximum light.

SPARKY

Echidnas pick up electrical currents through their noses!

YEP, THAT WAS AN ELECTRICAL STORM!

I KNOW WHERE YOU ARE!

13

BACK TO NATURE

Modern submarine sonar systems were inspired by bat and whale sonar. They send out a burst of sound then wait and listen for the echo. The target's location and distance can be calculated by working out the direction the echo came from and the length of time it took to return.

☐ sending out a short burst of sound

■ receiving echo

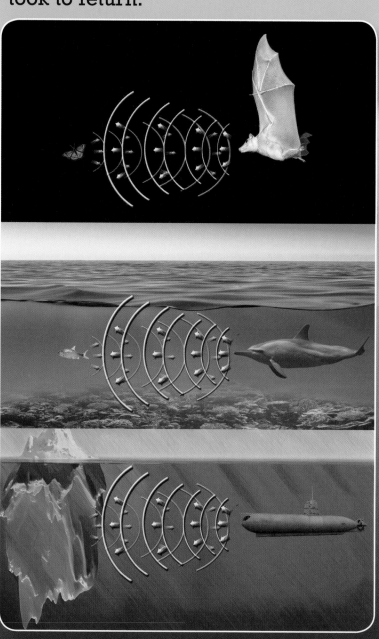

OILY-FACED GIANT

Do you know why sperm whales have such big heads? It's because they have two enormous, oil-filled sacs in their foreheads. No, it's not so they can fry up their dinner! It's part of their sonar system that helps them to locate food deep under the sea.

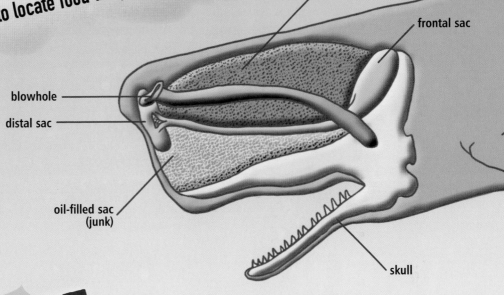

oil-filled sac (spermaceti organ)

frontal sac

blowhole

distal sac

oil-filled sac (junk)

skull

QUIET

PLEASE!

Can you guess the loudest animal sound on earth? It's not a lion's roar, or even the trumpet of an elephant, but a whale's clicking! A sperm whale's clicks are even louder than the sound of a jumbo jet taking off. Luckily it's quick, lasting only 1/10,000 of a second.

SNAP!

15

WHAT DID YOU SAY?

LOOK WITH YOUR EARS

Have you ever seen a movie where a bat flies into someone's hair? Well, it was probably science fiction! Although they fly around in the dark, bats rarely bump into things—including people! Bats use their ears to listen for the echoes of the ultrasonic clicks they make.

LISTEN UP

It's been said that blind people have a better sense of hearing than sighted people—but the truth is now known to be even more remarkable. It's been demonstrated that blind people can learn to echolocate! They can tell the difference between types of vehicles purely based on sound, even to the extent of distinguishing a front-wheel from a four-wheel drive.

SOUNDS LIKE TROUBLE!

FOOD BILL

If you put on a blindfold and blocked your ears, could you find your lunch? Maybe you could sniff it out, but the platypus has an amazing extra sense. Using their bills, they can detect the small electric currents emitted by their underwater prey.

SENSE OF PORPOISE

Dolphins have no sense of smell, but they can taste chemicals in the seawater they inhabit.

DID SOMEONE JUST PEE IN THE WATER?

Don't try this at home

In 1960, an experiment showed that dolphins with suction cups covering their eyes could navigate through a complicated maze. How did they do this? Through echolocation! Nice trick!

WHALES SING THE BLUES

Whales have signature frequencies that help scientists distinguish which species of whale is calling. Blue whales tend to call at frequencies between 15 and 20 hertz. Fin whales pulse at around 20 hertz, while humpbacks call out to each other at higher frequencies. But since 1992, US navy submarines have been detecting a whale song that doesn't fit with the others. It's a much higher 52 hertz, and its origins remain unknown. It's even been called the loneliest whale in the world!

TAIL LIGHTS

Here's another freaky sense—the olive sea snake's tail can sense light! There are special photosensitive areas on its tail that let the snake know if it's exposed. This means it can hide under a rock, safe in the knowledge that its tail isn't sticking out!

GOOD VIBES

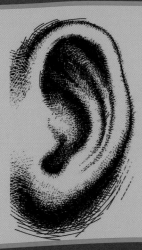

You've probably heard that snakes don't have ears. Yet somehow they can tell when their prey is approaching—by using their entire bodies to pick up vibrations from the air or ground. It's a bit like a snake antenna!

CALLING BIG BIRD

The lowest birdcalls ever recorded belong to the southern cassowary. Their deep rumble can travel long distances across the rainforest. Scientists think the horny bit on the bird's head can help it pick up calls from other cassowaries. Like mobile phones, only cheaper!

HELLO?

CHAPTER 3

FREAKY DESIGNS

If you could design an animal, what freaky features would you give it? Suction pads for feet? How about the ability to make light, goo or even glue? Sounds far-fetched—but they're all true!

GO ON... I DARE YA!

GOO SQUIRTERS

Golden-tailed geckos ooze goo from their bodies when predators threaten them. Even more dramatically, some geckos can eject a stream of gooey droplets over a distance of 1.6 feet (half a meter). That's a trick that only the snottiest of little brothers can manage! The goo has the consistency of thick honey, but turns into cobweb-like threads when it hits the predator.

THAT'S THE LAST TIME I TRY TO EAT A GECKO.

PUFFY, SPINY, STICKY, WHINING FROGS

AND FOR MY NEXT TRICK...

You wouldn't want to get in a fight with a giant burrowing frog. They get all puffed up, cover themselves in a white gluey substance and cry out like an off-key whining cat! And if that wasn't bad enough, the males have sharp spines on their thumbs, which they use to slice through the skin of their opponents! Ouch!

TAILS THAT SQUEAK

Like many lizards, the chameleon gecko drops its tail when threatened. But this bizarre animal has another trick up its tail! Once dropped, the tail doesn't just wriggle around on the ground—it also squeaks!

LIVING LIGHT

Amazingly, some animals can make light! This is known as bioluminescence. Most of these animals live deep in the ocean, where there isn't much sunlight. Some—such as fireflies and fungi—live on land. Bioluminescence is a cold light, meaning not much heat is given out.

LIGHT WAVES

Some sea animals put on a stunning light show. Dinoflagellates are a type of plankton and are so tiny they're almost invisible to the naked eye. They gather in warm-water lagoons or bays with narrow openings to the sea. When disturbed, they light up the water with dazzling blue flashes. They can even light up an entire lagoon!

THAT'S MORSE CODE FOR "I'M NOT HOME"!

FLASHY FISH

Flashlight fish have built-in lights that they can turn on and off! They produce sudden flashes of light to startle and confuse predators. The lights are large, white light organs under each eye, containing luminescent bacteria.

Just one scoop, thanks

Would you like to try glow-in-the-dark ice cream? What if it's jellyfish flavored? Chinese scientists have produced an ice cream made from the luminescent protein in jellyfish. The glow is triggered when the ice cream mixes with the acids in your mouth and the heat of your tongue. It's a bargain at just $225 a scoop!

BUILT-IN FISHING ROD

The anglerfish gets its name from the piece of spine that protrudes over its head and dangles like a fleshy, glowing lure in front of its mouth. The light draws prey within snatching distance, then the anglerfish snaps its mouth open and sucks up the victim before it knows what's happened!

THANKS FOR THE LIGHT!

FEATURES

small number of fins

dorsal appendage gives off light produced by symbiotic bacteria

sharp teeth for seizing prey

stomach can enlarge to fit big prey inside

A L. Clement

Interestingly, only female anglerfish possess the glowing lure. The male, which is much smaller by comparison, doesn't need one. He is a parasite and feeds off the female. When he finds a female, he bites into her with his sharp teeth and holds on!

WHERE THE SUN DON'T SHINE

The sun doesn't shine out of these creature's bottoms—they produce their own light! Glow-worms aren't really worms at all; they're actually fly larvae. Glow-worms live in caves and in rainforests. They build snares to lure and trap insects, a bit like spiders. Glow-worms produce light out of their bottoms, which attracts their prey like moths to a flame.

GLOW-WORM LIFE CYCLE

adult

eggs

pupa

glow-worm

FLASHY BOTTOMS

Fireflies sound exciting, but their name doesn't really fit—they don't produce fire, and they aren't even flies! Instead, they are beetles whose bottoms glow without giving off heat. Fireflies produce something known as cold light. The light grows brighter when they fly because more oxygen is being pumped to the muscles that make the light.

....• BATTERY
RUNNING
OUT...

CODED MESSAGES

There are 2,000 species of fireflies, but not all of them produce light. Of those that do, each has a unique pattern of flashes. This allows the fireflies to recognize other members of their species. Fireflies flash to help them find potential mates, but scientists aren't exactly sure how they do it!

REMOTE-CONTROLLED ROACHES

Instead of a remote-controlled car, how would you like a remote-controlled cockroach? Scientists are turning roaches into little robot zombies, wiring them up and controlling them with electrical signals. It's not just for the fun of it, though! One day, cockroaches with tiny cameras mounted on their backs may be sent into collapsed buildings to help search for survivors.

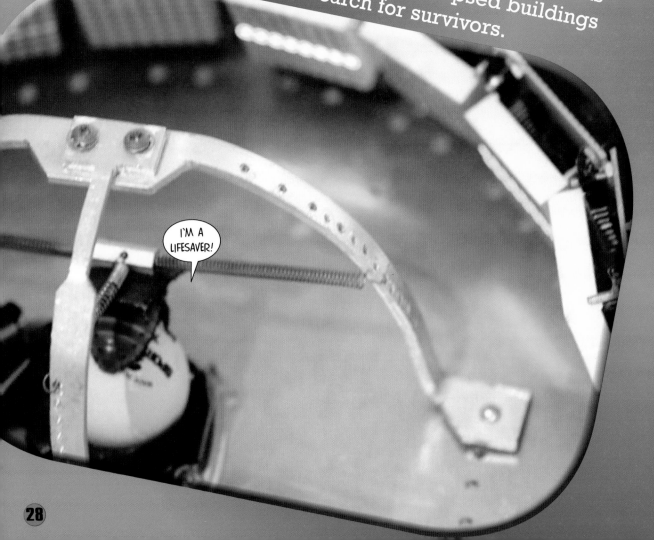

I'M A LIFESAVER!

MEDICAL MARVEL

The skin of a green tree-frog has some freaky properties. It is used as a post-surgery drug and as a treatment for some brain disorders. The magnificent tree-frog has a gland on its head that contains a mixture of 30 different chemicals that—apart from smelling like cashew nuts—may have even more bizarre properties!

IT MAKES ME NUTTY!

PIGEON VISION

Pigeons can see 340 degrees around them without turning their heads. That's almost a full circle! By comparison, humans can see about 180 degrees.

monocular vision   binocular vision

humans   owls   pigeons

STICKY FEET

What can scuttle upside down across the ceiling? Spiders, of course! Tree-frogs come close, and they can even climb up and down vertical walls. But geckos are the masters of hanging on. How do they do it? Through millions of tiny hairs on their toes, which stick to almost any material except Teflon—the nonstick coating in your frying pan. Though that doesn't mean you should try it with your stove on! Wouldn't that be a sticky situation?

HANGING ON

Tree-frogs are experts at clinging on to both wet and dry surfaces. The bottoms of their feet are covered with tiny bumps like cleats on the bottom of soccer shoes. These give tree-frogs good traction when they climb slippery surfaces.

A tree-frog's toe pads also have little channels that they use to control fluid depending on the surface. The channels funnel away excess water in wet conditions, and bring more fluid when the frog is on a dry or uneven surface that requires more suction for a tighter hold.

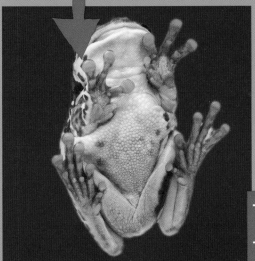

underside of frog's toe pad

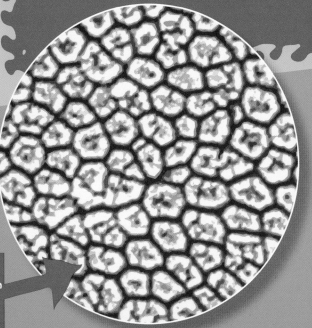

enlarged

CHAPTER 4

FREAKY Behavior

Animals develop weird behaviors to help them deal with the particular dangers they face. Some behaviors are so freaky that they'll make your classmates look normal!

NOTHING TO SEE HERE, I'M JUST AN EIGHT-LEGGED BIRD...

Asian Bronze-winged Jacana

SNEAKY SNORKELS

Jacana chicks have managed to find creative ways to hide from predators. They can hide in their father's wings so that only their legs stick out. They can also hide underwater. They poke their beaks above the surface and breathe, just like through a snorkel!

Australian Comb-crested Jacana

TOAD SAUSAGE

Scientists are trying to save the northern quolls—by making them sick! The endangered quolls are dying after eating toxic cane toads, which are invading their habitat in northern Australia. In response, scientists have developed a recipe for revolting cane toad sausages. They are made from minced cane toad legs and a tasteless chemical that makes the quolls sick. The scientists hope the quolls will come to associate the taste of cane toads with a turn of the stomach—and give up their deadly treat for good.

YECH!

WHISTLING SPIDER

Did you know bird-eating spiders can whistle? The sound is made by them rubbing their palps (between their front legs) along spines on their fangs. They do this when they feel threatened. If you ever hear it, take heed!

WHISTLE WHILE YOU WORK!

ARE YOU LOOKING AT ME?

The common spotted cuscus secretes a reddish-brown liquid around its eyes when it gets stressed that can look like blood oozing out!

BALD PATCH

Sloths may be famous for being lazy, but the cuscus must surely be its marsupial rival. It spends so much time sitting down that the fur on its bottom sometimes rubs off!

I'M GETTING A WIG...

Common Spotted Cuscus

UNSUSPECTING MOTH

FLAP
FLAP
FLAP
FLAP
FLAP

STICKY SITUATION

Not all spiders use webs to catch prey. The bolas spider gets its name from its weapon of choice—a single silken thread with a sticky ball on the end that resembles a South American throwing weapon called a bolas. The spider swings the bolas, luring moths to the sticky ball with its chemical perfume. The spider then pulls up the strand, and dinner is served!

CHAPTER 5

FREAKY BREEDING

We've all had moments when we've rolled our eyes in embarrassment at the crazy things our siblings and parents have done. But when it comes to relative reproduction, just be thankful you're not part of these freaky families!

BIG BROOD

Huntsman spider moms lay up to 200 eggs in one go. Once the eggs hatch, the babies stay on their mom's back for a few weeks. Remember that next time you reach for the bug spray!

I'M LIKE YOU! NOT REALLY

The name of the eclectus parrot is derived from the word "eclectic," which means from various sources. This is fitting, as the male is green and the female is red, which initially led observers to believe they were totally different species. Thank goodness they're not color blind!

TONS OF TOADS

Cane toads can pop out 350,000 eggs in one go. No wonder they're such a problem!

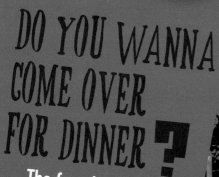

DO YOU WANNA COME OVER FOR DINNER?

The female praying mantis has a funny way of treating her partner. During mating, she's inclined to bite off his head and eat it!

MAYBE NOT...

COME FLY WITH ME

Male dragonflies aren't the most romantic creatures. If they see a female they'd like to mate with, they don't wait to be invited. They simply grab onto the back of her head and take off!

WHAT? NO FLOWERS?

stressed to death

Male antechinus only mate once in their entire lives. The experience is so stressful that their immune system breaks down and they die within two weeks of mating. Females can live longer—but not by much! Some manage to live long enough to raise a second litter.

HANGERS ON

Unlike other marsupials we're familiar with, antechinus don't have pouches. Instead, the babies hang off their mother's teats, hitching a ride on her underside!

BETTER HOP ONTO MY BIKE...

MOTOR MANIA

Not all frogs go ribbit. In fact, most don't! The mating call of the male motorbike frog sounds exactly like its name suggests— the revving of a motorbike! Like all boys and their toys, this frog's call is a matter of ego. He not only uses it to attract females but to compete with other males!

LITTLE MONSTERS

GIVE ME FOOD, NOW!

Shearwater chicks feed heavily for 10 weeks after hatching and can end up weighing twice as much as their parents!

I HOPE YOU LIKE BLUE...

Satin bowerbird males could get jobs as interior designers! The birds have striking blue eyes, which they match with blue objects they collect from their environment. These include man-made objects, such as plastic bottle tops and pegs. The males arrange the objects around a stick display called a bower to attract females.

CLINGY RELATIONSHIPS

The male anglerfish takes clingy to a whole new level. When he wants to mate, he bites onto the much larger female—and never lets go! Their circulatory systems are fused together, and all the male's organs shut down except for his reproductive system.

LIZARD LOVE

Spring is the season of love for male blue-tongue lizards, who will pursue females in order to mate. But lizard courtship can be a rough affair, and sometimes a female can end up with scrape marks from a male's teeth!

WHAT WAS THAT?

Finding a partner requires very little effort for some female spiders. The males of their species are so small in comparison that they can even mate without the female noticing! Talk about a blind date!

CHAPTER 6

FREAKY BABIES

Remember the saying, "A face only a mother could love"? No, we're not talking about your little brother or sister! Spare a thought for the parents of these odd animal babies. Whether it's the way they were born or the way they behave, these newborn creatures sure are freaky!

YOU FORGOT MY BIRTHDAY PRESENT!

DRATTED RATS

Poor black rats—they don't live long enough to enjoy their first birthdays. But they certainly make the most of their short lives. Black rats manage to make 60–100 baby rats in less than 12 months!

POPPING THEM OUT

You might think rabbits make babies quickly, but that's nothing compared to bandicoots. Rabbits can make a baby from go to whoa in 30 days. House mice can do it 18–21 days. But the bandicoot takes only 12.5 days! They can produce a litter every two months. That means 48 new baby bandicoots each year!

MILKING THEIR PARENTS

It's not strictly true that only mammals produce milk. Pigeons do too! It's produced in their crops—a pouch near the throat used to store food—and it looks like cottage cheese. And it's made by both the moms and the dads!

DOUBLE TROUBLE

Kangaroos can suckle two young at once, even when they're different ages! The nipple used by the newborn provides milk that is practically fat free. Older joeys need more nourishment, so their milk contains 20 percent fat.

CHOCOLATE OR VANILLA?

POCKET-SIZED BABIES

The terrestrial hip pocket frog literally has pockets on its hips! But instead of carrying loose change, the pockets have a much more important use. After hatching, the tadpoles wriggle into pouch openings on either side of the male's body and stay there until they develop into froglets.

YELLOW GREEN SNAKES

Guess what color green tree pythons are when they hatch? Easy question, right? Wrong! When the pythons first hatch they are actually bright yellow. They spend their first year mainly hunting on the ground in open rainforest. It's only once they start hunting in the trees that they change to their distinctive green color.

IT'S NOT EASY BEING YELLOW...

HAMMERED AT BIRTH

The strangely shaped head of the hammerhead shark is far too big for an easy birth, especially when Mom is giving birth to up to 40 pups! The heads of hammerhead pups are soft and fold back as they exit the birth canal then stiffen up shortly after they are born.

IS IT HOT IN HERE?

Imagine if the sex of your child were determined by temperature. Incredibly, this is the case for estuarine crocodile hatchlings! If the nest is 88–91°F (31– 33 °C), then all the hatchlings will be boys. If it's above or below this temperature, the hatchlings will all be girls! No matter the sex, the eggs are precious to their mothers. Many are exposed by rainfall washing away the nests. The surviving hatchlings are carried to the water and guarded by the mother crocodile for up to two months.

MOMMY!

45

THAT'S FREAKY!

luminescent	something that shines in the dark or reflects light well
lure	something that attracts
parasite	a plant or animal that lives in or on another plant or animal and then feeds on it
protrude	something that sticks out
pursue	to follow something in order to catch it
regulate	to control or change something so that a standard is met
secrete	to leak out a substance from the body
snare	a trap
take heed	to pay attention to something or notice it
temperament	the way a person is naturally or the type of personality he or she has
terrestrial	when something lives on land rather than in the sea or sky
toxic	something poisonous that can cause sickness or even death
unique	to be different from all others
withstand	to hold firm against something and resist it

Additional images:

A.L. Clement: p. 25 (anglerfish engraving) *Deep Sea Angler (Melanocetus johnsonii)* (Plate 23) from *Living lights: a popular account of phosphorescent animals and vegetables* by Charles Frederick Holder, 1887, London: Sampson Low, Marston; Greg Harold/AUSCAPE: p. 21 (chameleon gecko); Greg Harm: p. 40 (satin bowerbird eye); Garnet Hertz: p. 28 (cockroach controlled mobile robot); Markrosenrosen: p. 26 (glow-worm cave) *Glowworm (Arachnocampa luminosa) in a cave in New Zealand*/CC BY-SA 4.0, http://commons.wikimedia.org/wiki/File:Nz_glowworm.jpeg; Ian Morris: pp. 6 (green tree-frog without eye), 21 (giant burrowing frog), 37 (mass of cane toad toadlets), 39 (male motorbike frog) & 44 (green tree python); Markus Nolf: p. 26 (glow-worm larvae) *Two larvae of Arachnocampa luminosa with snares*/CC BY-SA 2.0, http://commons.wikimedia.org/wiki/File:Arachnocampa_luminosa_larvae.jpg; NORFANZ Founding Parties/Kerryn Parkinson: p. 5 (blobfish) *Blobfish, genus Psychrolutes microporos*, AMS I.42771-001; Pete Oxford/naturepl.com: p. 4 (giant Titicaca Lake frog); T. Jeffrey Parker: front cover (medical leech) *Head of Hirudo medicinalis* (Fig. 118a) from *A Manual of Zoology*, 1900, New York, NY: The MacMillan Company; Catherine Prentice: p. 9 (albino Bennett's wallaby); Queensland Museum: p. 44 (terrestrial hip pocket frog); The Royal Society: p.31 (underside of frog's toe pad enlarged and enlarged more) *Scanning electron microscopies of frog toe pad and high power view of the surface of a single hexagonal cell showing peg-like projections* (Fig. 1) from 'Wet but not slippery: boundary friction in tree frog adhesive toe pads' by W. Federle, W.J.P. Barnes, W. Baumgartner, P. Drechsler and J.M. Smith, October 2006: The Royal Society; Forest & Kim Starr: p. 39 (shearwater chick) *Shearwater chick*/CC BY 2.0, https://www.flickr.com/photos/starr-environmental/10789319083; Ken Stepnell: p. 10 (emperor gum moth); Jed Sundwall: p. 22 (dinoflagellates) *Bioluminescence*/CC BY-SA 2.0, https://www.flickr.com/photos/12859704@N00/74363235/; Valerie Taylor: pp. 15 (sperm whale calf), 23 (flashlight fish) & 41 (male anglerfish).

Licences:

http://creativecommons.org/licenses/by/2.0/
http://creativecommons.org/licenses/by-sa/2.0/
http://creativecommons.org/licenses/by-sa/2.0/deed.en
http://creativecommons.org/licenses/by-sa/4.0/